JULIETTE'S
SPECULOOS

JULIETTE'S
SPECULOOS

Recipes from Bruges' most charming biscuit bakery

BRENDA KEIRSEBILCK
PHOTOGRAPHY BY KAREN VAN WINKEL

LANNOO

FOREWORD

I have always enjoyed baking. As an 8-year old I began with a simple sponge cake from one of my grandmother's recipe books. This was followed by apple and rice tarts, flans and frangipane. I found it fascinating just how many things you could cook from flour, sugar, butter and eggs, simply by using different quantities and working them in different ways.

Despite my love of cooking, I ended up not in the bakery world but in the wonderful world of advertising. For fifteen years I worked for all kinds of customers and products and travelled the world. The souvenirs I brought back from my travels were spices, fruits, typical local ingredients, cookery books, half of which I could not understand, and piles of photos of all the delicious things you find in shop windows. My general memories of most of these places have long disappeared, but I have precise memories of many of the delicious things I ate there.

At a certain juncture I decided to follow a three-year bakery course, not with the idea of doing anything particular with it, but as a sort of counterweight to the stress of my job. The end of this training coincided with a badly needed sabbatical that I had inserted into my career, and then the baking virus hit me full force.

During my travels, the cupcake craze in the States and the United Kingdom had not escaped me, and it's here that I took my first plunge, travelling for two weeks to England to spend time with pastry chefs acquiring the intricacies of royal icing and sugarcraft. I learned to model sugar-paste flowers and produce *pastillage* decorations. Very interesting, but too much focus on decoration and not enough on taste. This was not the direction I wanted to take.

Shortly after that my husband and I went for a three months sailing trip to Brittany and I took it upon myself to decide during the trip whether I would go back to advertising or start something new, tabula rasa, 'something to do with baking'. Brittany stole my heart. In each port we sailed into I jumped out of the boat as fast as I could to go on a raid. My booty: *caramel beurre salé, friands, macarons, Far Breton, kouign amann...* Many times, when staying several days in one port, we hired a car and travelled from one *biscuiterie artisanale* to another.

It was clear it would be 'something to do with biscuits'. Upon my return I very quickly took over Juliette's, a traditional biscuit bakery in the heart of Bruges. That was two years ago, and today I work hard every day with my wonderful team to provide our customers with a wide range of products, from classic dessert biscuits to cupcakes and even *whoopie pies*.

Every day when I enter my shop and studio, I smell what are for me still wonderful odours and I realize how lucky I am to be able to do what I do. And my biscuits? Now it's they, instead of me, that travel the world.

Brenda Keirsebilck

SPECULOOS

Speculoos (or also speculaas), a type of spiced biscuit from the gingerbread family, is extremely popular in Belgium, Netherlands and Germany. In the Netherlands and Germany you will find it in the shops only in December, whereas in Belgium it is purchased and eaten the whole year round. More than that: if we had to elect a national biscuit, speculoos would almost certainly be the winner.
Thanks in particular to Belgium's Lotus brand, this biscuit has become popular beyond our borders, often as 'Dutch windmill cookies' or 'airline cookies'. In the States speculoos biscuits are sold under the Biscoff brand name.
Speculoos biscuits have been around for hundreds of years, but it is only in recent years that we have seen a genuine revival. As a result they are today more hip than ever, and used for much more than simply accompanying a cup of coffee.
In our shop we bake a whole range of varieties, for which you will find the recipes in the first part of this book. In the second part we use the various speculoos biscuits as ingredients in preparing desserts.

Spices
The name speculoos refers to a mixture of spices. For 50 g speculoos spices you can mix 4 g pepper, 4 g ginger, 8 g cloves, 8 g nutmeg, 24 g cinnamon and 2 g cardamom. You can make it milder by adding more cinnamon, and sharper with more nutmeg and pepper. Aniseed, mace or coriander seeds can also be added.

Use of a wooden mould
'Dutch windmill cookie' refers to one of the many shapes that a speculoos biscuit can have. A wooden mould is used to give the biscuit its desired shape and its distinctive relief design. Of course you can shape the biscuit in any mould you want, and do not specially have to go out and purchase a wooden one. If you want to work with a wooden mould, then – to avoid the dough sticking to it – you must grease the new mould a few days before with neutral vegetable oil and then allow it to dry thoroughly. After that you should use sufficient flour every time before placing the dough in the mould. After taking the speculoos out of the mould and placing it on a baking tray, remove the excess flour from the dough with a little brush. Obviously you do not put the wooden mould into the oven.

Storing speculoos biscuits
Speculoos biscuits remain nice and crispy in a hermetically sealed container, preferably a tin.
If, despite this, the biscuits have gone soft, you can place them in a hot oven for a very short while to make the moisture disappear.

TABLE OF CONTENTS

Foreword – 4
Speculoos – 6

basic recipes
Speculoos biscuits – 12
Vanilla speculoos biscuits – 14
Soft speculoos biscuits – 17
Coffee speculoos biscuits – 18
Wholemeal speculoos biscuits – 20
Almond speculoos biscuits – 23
Lemon speculoos biscuits – 24
Ginger speculoos biscuits – 26
Speculoos with almond filling – 29
Speculoos paste with caramel taste – 31
Speculoos paste with white chocolate – 32

superb speculoos recipes
Speculoos muffins with cream cheese – 38
Speculoos meringues – 41
Tiramisu with speculoos – 43
Chocolate-coated marshmallows – 44
Speculoos mousse – 46
Luxury speculoos biscuits – 48
Far Breton with soft speculoos – 51
Banana and speculoos cake – 52
Edible Christmas tree – 54
White chocolate and speculoos truffles – 57
Vanilla and speculoos pudding – 58
Speculoos cream puffs – 60
Frangipane and speculoos tarts – 63

Marzipan and speculoos cakelets – 64

Speculoos tart on a cheese base – 66

Speculoos and lime slice – 69

Cup cakes with speculoos topping – 70

Speculoos and banana cakes – 73

Speculoos mousse with vanilla and whipped chocolate cream – 74

Speculoos kramiek – 76

Lemon meringue tart – 79

Speculoos risotto – 80

Speculoos ice cream cupcakes – 82

Layered meringue tart – 84

Apple tartlets with speculoos – 87

Speculoos paste cakes – 88

Speculoos macaroons – 90

Speculoos and white chocolate tart – 93

Speculoos and caramel cake – 94

Speculoos and curd cheese bavarois with raspberry coulis – 96

Speculoos whoopies – 98

Coffee-coated speculoos sponge cake – 100

Happy ginger cake – 103

Speculoos cheesecake – 104

Speculoos bread pudding – 106

Speculoos butter cream biscuits – 108

Speculoos and pear syrup tart – 111

Speculoos fudge – 112

Orange cakes – 114

Speculoos butter pancakes – 116

shopping list – 119

BASIC RECIPES

SPECULOOS BISCUITS

FOR 2.2 KG OF DOUGH

400 g butter
500 g brown sugar
200 g demerara sugar
1 egg
50 ml water
1 kg flour
10 g baking powder
10 g speculoos spices

- Soften the butter.
- Add the sugar and mix well.
- Beat in the egg.
- Add the water and mix again well.
- Sift the flour with the baking powder and spices onto the dough.
- Knead everything into a crumbly dough.
- Roll the dough into a ball and cover with plastic foil.
- Leave the dough to rest overnight in the refrigerator.
- Preheat the oven to 180 °C.
- Roll out the dough to 4 mm thick and shape the biscuits with a mould.
- Place on a tray lined with baking paper and bake for about 14 minutes. The baking time depends on the thickness of the biscuit. Push the centre of the biscuit and when it rises back, it's ready.
- Leave to cool before removing from the baking tray. Speculoos is still soft when it comes out of the oven and becomes hard only on cooling.

This dough can be perfectly divided into portions for freezing. Wrap it well in plastic foil and take it out of the freezer the day before, to allow it to thaw gently. Knead once again before using.

VANILLA SPECULOOS

A crunchy alternative for summer time.

FOR 1.6 KG OF DOUGH

300 g butter
500 g demerara sugar
1 egg
1 coffee spoon vanilla extract
75 ml water
700 g flour
10 g baking powder
1 pinch of salt
1 coffee spoon of ground vanilla powder

- Soften the butter.
- Add the sugar, egg and vanilla extract and mix well.
- Add the water gradually, beating it into the dough.
- Sift the flour, baking powder, salt and vanilla powder onto the mixture.
- Knead briefly into a crumbly dough.
- Roll the dough into a ball and cover with plastic foil.
- Leave the dough to rest overnight.
- Preheat the oven to 160 °C.
- Roll out the dough to 4 mm thick and shape the biscuits with a mould.
- Place on a tray lined with baking paper and bake for about 14 minutes. The baking time depends on the thickness of the biscuit. Push the centre of the biscuit and when it rises back, it's ready.
- Speculoos is still soft when it comes out of the oven and becomes hard only on cooling.

This dough can be perfectly divided into portions for freezing. Wrap it well in plastic foil and take it out of the freezer the day before, to allow it to thaw gently. Knead once again before using.

SOFT SPECULOOS

Adding almonds keeps this speculoos soft, as well as giving it a very particular taste. Keep the biscuits preferably in a closed plastic box and eat within two weeks.

FOR 20 BISCUITS

275 g butter
450 g dark muscovado sugar
3 g speculoos spices
3 g cinnamon
1 egg
100 ml water
750 g flour
11 g baking powder
125 g finely ground almonds
50 g almond shavings

- Blend together the butter, sugar, spices and cinnamon into a smooth mixture.
- Add the egg and water and mix well again.
- Add the flour, baking powder and ground almonds and mix briefly into a homogeneous dough.
- Finally, add the sliced almonds and mix again briefly.
- Shape the dough into a large roll, wrap in plastic foil and leave to rest for at least 4 hours.
- Cut slices about 1.5 cm thick (about 90 grams) and flatten them lightly.
- Bake at 180 °C for 24 minutes.

COFFEE SPECULOOS BISCUITS

FOR 2.3 KG OF DOUGH

400 g butter
500 g dark muscovado sugar
200 g demerara sugar
10 g baking powder
1 egg
50 ml water
10 ml coffee extract
1 kg flour
10 g speculoos spices
100 g almond shavings

- Soften the butter.
- Add the sugar and mix well.
- Beat in the egg.
- Add the water and the coffee extract and mix well.
- Sift the flour with the baking powder and spices onto the dough.
- Knead everything into a crumbly dough.
- Mix the almonds briefly into the dough.
- Roll the dough into a ball and cover with plastic foil.
- Leave the dough to rest overnight in the refrigerator.
- Preheat the oven to 180 °C.
- Roll the dough till 4 mm thick and press out the shapes.
- Place onto a baking tray lined with baking paper and bake for about 14 minutes.
- Leave to cool before removing from the baking tray.
- The baking time depends on the thickness of the biscuit.
- Push the centre of the biscuit and when it rises back, it's ready.
- Speculoos is still soft when it comes out of the oven and becomes hard only on cooling.

This dough can be perfectly divided into portions for freezing. Wrap it well in plastic foil and take it out of the freezer the day before, to allow it to thaw gently. Knead once again before using.

WHOLEMEAL SPECULOOS BISCUITS

The bran and the wholemeal flour give the speculoos biscuit a very special taste.

FOR 30 BISCUITS

100 g butter at room temperature
85 g white sugar
15 g honey
3 teaspoons baking powder
1.5 coffee spoon speculoos spices
2 tablespoons milk
200 g wholemeal flour
35 g bran

- Blend together the butter, sugar, spices and cinnamon into a homogeneous mixture.
- Work in the milk, and then the honey.
- Lastly, knead in the flour and bran thoroughly.
- Wrap the dough in foil and leave to rest overnight.
- Roll out the dough till 4 mm thick and press out the shapes.
- Preheat the oven to 170 °C.
- Roll the dough out 4 mm thick and shape the biscuits with a mould.
- Place on a baking tray lined with baking paper and bake for about 12 minutes. The baking time depends on the thickness of the biscuit.
- Push the centre of the biscuit and when it rises back, it's ready.
- Leave to cool before removing from the baking tray.
- Speculoos is still soft when it comes out of the oven and becomes hard only on cooling.

ALMOND SPECULOOS

FOR 2.25 KG OF DOUGH

500 g butter
500 g demerara sugar
2 teaspoons cinnamon
1 pinch of salt
3 eggs
5 g baking powder
700 g flour
375 g almond shavings

- Soften the butter.
- Add the sugar, cinnamon and salt and blend well.
- Add the eggs and beat well.
- Sift the flour and baking powder and mix into the dough.
- Carefully knead in the almond shavings by hand right through the dough.
- Roll the dough into a ball and cover with plastic foil.
- Leave the dough to rest overnight.
- Preheat the oven to 180 °C.
- Divide the dough ball into quarters and roll out each piece into a sausage shape.
- Cut into 4 mm thick slices and lay on a baking tray lined with a baking sheet.
- Bake for about 12 minutes. The baking time depends on the thickness of the biscuit.
- Push the centre of the biscuit and when it rises back, it's ready.
- Leave to cool before removing from the baking tray.
- Speculoos is still soft when it comes out of the oven and becomes hard only on cooling.

This dough can be perfectly divided into portions for freezing. Wrap well in plastic foil and take it out of the freezer the day before, to allow it to thaw gently. Knead once again before using.

LEMON SPECULOOS

The fresh lemon combines surprisingly with the speculoos spices.

FOR 1 KG OF DOUGH

200 g butter at room temperature
250 g demerara sugar
20 g lemon zest
2 g ground vanilla
450 g flour
7 g baking powder
1 egg
10 g lemon juice
10 g milk

- Mix the butter with the demerara sugar, lemon zest and vanilla.
- Sift the flour with the baking powder and add to the butter mixture.
- Beat in the egg, the lemon juice, and last of all the milk.
- Shape the dough into a ball and cover with plastic foil.
- Leave to rest at least overnight.
- Preheat the oven to 160 °C.
- Roll out the dough to 4 mm thick. Cut out the desired shape and place on a baking tray lined with baking paper.
- Bake for 10 to 15 minutes, depending on the size of the biscuits.
- The baking time depends on the thickness of the biscuit.
- Press the centre of the biscuit and when it rises back, it's ready.
- Leave to cool before removing from the baking tray.
- Speculoos is still soft when it comes out of the oven and becomes hard only on cooling.

Tip: the milk can be completely replaced by lemon juice if desired.

This dough can be perfectly divided into portions for freezing. Wrap well in plastic foil and take it out of the freezer the day before, to allow it to thaw gently. Knead once again before using.

GINGER SPECULOOS

This taste is rather similar to ginger snaps, but with the typical structure and crunch of traditional speculoos biscuits.

FOR 1.5 KG OF DOUGH

300 g butter
500 g demerara sugar
2 eggs
20 g ginger powder
665 g flour
6 g baking powder

- Blend the butter and sugar with the mixer into a homogenous mixture.
- Add the eggs and ginger powder.
- Sift the flour with the baking powder and mix with the rest.
- Leave the dough to rest overnight.
- Preheat the oven to 180 °C.
- Roll out the dough to about 5 millimetres thick and cut out into circles.
- Bake for 17 minutes. The baking time depends on the thickness of the biscuit.
- Press the speculoos in the centre, and when it rises back, it's ready.
- Leave to cool before removing from the baking tray. Speculoos is still soft when it comes out of the oven and becomes hard only on cooling.

This dough can be perfectly divided into portions for freezing. Wrap well in plastic foil and take it out of the freezer the day before, to allow it to thaw gently. Knead once again before using.

SPECULOOS WITH ALMOND FILLING

FOR A 20 X 20 CM BAKING TIN

For the speculoos
125 g butter
125 g dark muscovado sugar
25 ml milk
1 egg
5 g baking powder
7 g speculoos spices
1 pinch of salt
250 g flour

For the filling
100 g butter
100 g sugar
100 g ground almonds.
2 eggs
40 g flour

For the finishing
1 egg
chopped almonds

- Mix the butter with the sugar.
- Add the milk, egg, baking powder, spices and salt.
- Then knead in the flour.
- Shape the dough into a big block, cover with foil and place for at least 12 hours in the refrigerator.
- For the filling, beat the butter and sugar together until white.
- Add the ground almonds.
- Add the eggs one by one, beating well each time.
- Once everything is well combined, add the flour.
- Preheat the oven to 170 °C.
- Divide the speculoos dough into two halves and roll out each half 1 cm thick.
- Spread one half with the almond filling.
- Place the other half carefully on top of the filling.
- Brush the top with egg and sprinkle with chopped almonds.
- Bake for 1 hour, turning once halfway through.
- Allow to cool completely before cutting the speculoos.

SPECULOOS PASTE WITH CARAMEL TASTE

FOR 2 JARS

1 can condensed milk (397 g)
speculoos spices
20 g speculoos (optional)

- Mix the spices gradually into the condensed milk until it tastes right.
- Heat up over a low heat, but continue stirring to prevent the milk burning. The longer you let the milk boil, the darker the colour and the stronger the caramel taste.
- (Optional) Crumble the speculoos and stir it into the paste.
- Pour into heat-proof jars and leave to cool before closing.
- This paste keeps for two weeks in the refrigerator.

A delicious alternative to peanut butter.

SPECULOOS PASTE WITH WHITE CHOCOLATE

Delicious on hot toast or pancakes, the chocolate melts away, leaving the crunchy speculoos.

FOR 4 JARS

1 dl cream
500 g granulated sugar
20 g glucose*
20 g butter
165 g white chocolate
3 speculoos biscuits of 10 g each
8 g speculoos spices

- Put the cream, sugar and glucose in a pan and bring to the boil.
- Remove from heat.
- Add the butter and the chocolate and mix well.
- Crumble and add the speculoos biscuits.
- Mix in the spices gradually and taste until the taste is right.
- Pour the paste into fireproof jars and leave to cool before closing.
- This paste can be kept for two weeks without refrigeration.

* *Glucose is sold in bakeries and pharmacies.*

SUPERB SPECULOOS RECIPES
───────────

SPECULOOS MUFFINS WITH CREAM CHEESE

I once tasted in Denmark a carrot tart topped with cream cheese and found it so distinctive that at home I spread cream cheese over my speculoos muffins. A perfect match ... Add a few roasted almonds and you're away!

FOR 12 MUFFINS

For the muffins
60 g dark muscovado sugar
65 g granulated sugar
125 g butter at room temperature
125 g self-raising flour
2 eggs
2 tablespoons full-fat milk
1 soft speculoos biscuit, crumbled

For the cream cheese topping
80 g soft butter at room temperature
125 g cream cheese
300 g icing sugar
almond shavings
1 pinch of cinnamon

- Preheat the oven to 160 °C.
- Blend together the sugar and the butter with the mixer into an smooth mixture.
- Add the flour and blend for another 30 seconds.
- Add the eggs and the milk, and continue blending until you have a homogeneous mixture.
- Finally, using a spatula, incorporate the crumbled speculoos into the dough.
- Grease a muffin tin and fill evenly with the dough.
- Bake the muffins for about 23 minutes (check using a wooden skewer).
- Allow to cool.
- For the topping, mix the butter and cream cheese on a medium speed setting and then add the icing sugar spoon by spoon.
- Beat briefly at a high speed setting to make the topping light and airy.
- Cut the cooled muffins across and spread thickly with a layer of cream cheese.
- Mix the icing sugar with water to a stiff dressing and pour over the muffins.
- Fry the sliced almonds with a little cinnamon in a hot pan.
- Sprinkle them over the muffins and serve immediately.

SPECULOOS MERINGUES

FOR 10 CAKES

2 egg whites
1 pinch of speculoos spices
125 g granulated sugar

- Preheat the oven to 100 °C.
- Beat the egg whites until stiff in an absolutely fat-free bowl.
- Mix the speculoos spices with the sugar.
- Add the sugar mixture spoonful by spoonful to the egg white and continue beating till it peaks.
- Spoon the mixture carefully into a pastry bag and place little blobs onto a baking tray lined with baking paper.
- Bake the meringues for 2 hours in the oven; then turn off the oven, but leave the meringues inside until the oven cools.
- Decorate with grated speculoos biscuit crumbs.

Tip: for dark meringues, use dark muscovado instead of granulated sugar.

TIRAMISU WITH SPECULOOS

My husband has been making this particular version of tiramisu for years. He sometimes adds another layer of banana to it or replaces the Baileys with advocaat.

FOR 4 PORTIONS

2 eggs
50 g icing sugar
1 spirit glass of Baileys
250 g mascarpone
strong cold coffee
speculoos biscuits, around 4 mm thick *(see recipe on p. 12)*

- Separate the eggs and beat the egg whites until stiff.
- Mix the egg yolks with the icing sugar and Baileys.
- Add the mascarpone and mix until smooth.
- Fold the beaten egg whites gently into the mixture.
- Pour the coffee into a soup bowl and dunk the speculoos biscuits right in (but don't let them absorb the coffee or they'll become far too soft).
- Place a biscuit at the bottom of a glass and spoon in a layer of cream on top.
- Continue in this way until the glasses are full, ending with a layer of cream.
- Place for at least 4 hours in the refrigerator.
- Crumble the remaining speculoos biscuits and add just before serving.

CHOCOLATE-COATED MARSHMALLOWS

To avoid the biscuit part being softened by the egg white mixture, we always first dunk it into the chocolate. For a nice glossy chocolate coating, it is important to get the chocolate to the right temperature.

FOR 25 MARSHMALLOWS

625 g chocolate
25 speculoos biscuits, 4 mm thick
    (see recipe on p. 12)
almond shavings
honey
225 g granulated sugar
75 ml water
110 g egg white
1 leaf gelatine

- Melt two thirds of the chocolate in a bain-marie.
- Then add the remaining chocolate and stir well until completely melted.
- Dunk the speculoos biscuits in the chocolate and leave to dry on a sheet of baking paper.
- Caramelize the almond shavings with the honey and place a layer on each biscuit.
- Boil the sugar and water to 120 °C.
- Beat the egg white until it holds peaks.
- Soak the gelatin in cold water and add it to the sugar solution.
- Continue to beat the egg white and add the boiling sugar spoonful by spoonful.
- Continue to beat until the egg white has cooled.
- Spray little blobs on the biscuits using a pastry bag.
- Place for a few hours in the refrigerator.
- Re-heat the chocolate in the bain-marie and stir until it has cooled to 32 °C.
- Dunk the marshmallows in the chocolate and place back on the baking paper.
- Leave to cool.

SPECULOOS MOUSSE

This mousse is easy to make and you can vary it endlessly. If you want, you can replace half the cream with mascarpone or cheese. Use one of the two types of caramelized biscuit spread from this book (see recipes on p. 31 and 32) or both together.

FOR 4 PORTIONS

2 eggs
1 large tablespoon sugar
3 tablespoons speculoos paste
200 ml cream (at least 40% fat)
20 g ground speculoos

- Separate the eggs.
- Beat the egg whites until stiff and set aside.
- Mix the egg yolks with the sugar and beat firmly.
- Heat up the speculoos paste evenly so that it is liquid, stir well and leave to cool.
- Beat the cream to a thick liquid consistency and fold into the egg yolk mixture.
- Then stir in the speculoos paste firmly.
- Add the crumbled speculoos biscuits.
- Finally fold the egg white carefully into the mixture.
- Pour the mousse into glasses or cups and leave for at least 1 hour in the refrigerator.

LUXURY SPECULOOS BISCUITS

A few little additions turn an ordinary speculoos biscuit into a luxury item.

---

100 g white chocolate
speculoos biscuits, 4 mm thick
  (see recipe on p. 12)

- Melt the white chocolate in a bain-marie.
- Dip the tops of the speculoos biscuits into the chocolate and leave to harden on a piece of baking paper.
- Crumble a speculoos biscuit and add some crumbs into the chocolate before it is completely hard.

There are endless possible variations. Some ideas:
  * *Mix some lemon or lime juice into the chocolate.*
  * *Mix icing sugar with water to give a thick icing.*
  * *Sprinkle with chocolate chips or coloured sugar balls.*
  * *Spread speculoos paste with caramel onto a biscuit and cover with a second biscuit.*

FAR BRETON WITH SOFT SPECULOOS

France is one of my favourite vacation destinations, not least because the country has so many specialties that particularly appeal to my taste buds. In Brittany, for example, the Far Breton, a sort of flan with soaked prunes, is not to be despised. In this recipe I have added below a base of speculoos biscuit and replaced the plums with pieces of soft speculoos biscuit.

50 g butter
100 g ground speculoos
250 g sugar
250 g flour
6 eggs
1 litre full-fat milk.
3 soft speculoos biscuits

- Preheat the oven to 170 °C.
- Melt the butter and mix with the ground speculoos.
- Distribute the mixture over the bottom of a greased baking tin and press down well with the back of a spoon.
- Place for five minutes in the oven and then leave to cool.
- Mix the sugar with the flour.
- Add the eggs one by one, beating well each time.
- Continue to beat the mixture for a further 10 minutes or so.
- Meanwhile, heat the milk until almost boiling.
- Pour one third of the hot milk into the mixture and beat well.
- Add the rest of the milk bit by bit, continuing to beat thoroughly.
- If necessary re-grease the sides of the baking tin.
- Ladle the mixture carefully into the tin (don't pour, or the speculoos base will come away).
- Break the soft speculoos into large pieces and place in the mixture.
- Bake the far for 50 minutes.
- Serve lukewarm or cold.

SPECULOOS AND BANANA CAKE

I first ate banana cake in Costa Rica. It's the perfect snack, if you want with a layer of creamy butter on top.

120 g butter	• Preheat the oven to 180 °C.
120 g sugar	• Line a rectangular baking tin with baking paper.
2 eggs	• Cream the butter and sugar together.
100 g flour	• Beat in the eggs well.
1 teaspoon baking powder	• Sift the flour and baking powder into the dough.
1 teaspoon speculoos spices	• Mix all ingredients well.
60 g wholemeal flour	• Add the speculoos spices and the wholemeal flour and mix well.
3 large bananas	• Mash the bananas and fold into the dough.
70 g ground speculoos	• Finally, add the speculoos crumbs and fold in briefly.
	• Spoon the mixture into the tin and bake for 60 minutes.

Tip: add some chopped walnuts for an even richer flavour.

EDIBLE CHRISTMAS TREE

This tree can be made a few days before Christmas and placed on the table as a Christmas decoration.

For the tree
1 kilo normal speculoos dough
   (see recipe on p. 12)

For the decoration
350 g icing sugar
30 g egg white
green food dye (preferably in gel form) for the green tree

- Preheat the oven to 180 °C.
- Draw stars from small to large on pieces of paper and cut them out.
- Roll out the dough to 5 mm thick.
- Place the paper stars onto the dough and cut along the edges with a knife.
- Cut two copies of each size star in the dough.
- Bake first the smallest stars for 15 minutes.
- Then bake the biggest stars for 18 minutes.

- Place the icing sugar in a bowl and mix slowly.
- Add the egg white slowly, beating all the time.
- Gradually increase the mixing speed.
- Continue beating until the egg white icing is stiff and forms peaks.
- Add some water, a few drops at a time, and stir well until the icing is spreadable, but absolutely not runny. For the green tree, add the green colouring.
- Spread a little icing in the middle of the largest star and also decorate the points of the star.
- Place the next star on top and repeat until all the stars have been used up.
- Decorate the Christmas tree with silver balls and leave to dry.

WHITE CHOCOLATE AND SPECULOOS TRUFFLES

Bruges has the largest concentration of chocolate shops in the world and truffles are hugely popular, so this is a perfect marriage of the two specialties.

FOR 25 TRUFFLES

150 g white chocolate
50 g butter
1 dash of Cointreau (optional)
100 g finely ground speculoos

- Melt the chocolate in a bain-marie.
- Beat the butter until airy.
- Spread the chocolate over the butter and mix with a spatula.
- Add the Cointreau.
- Using two spoons, place small balls of the mixture on a tray lined with baking paper.
- Place the truffles in the refrigerator to stiffen.
- Place the crushed speculoos into a soup plate.
- Just before serving, roll the stiffened truffles through the speculoos crumbs.

VANILLA AND SPECULOOS PUDDING

If there is a dessert from my childhood that always brings back sweet memories, this is it. When we came home from school and there was a yellow pudding with speculoos waiting for us, it was always a party. Now my mother has grandchildren she makes it again, so I simply had to include it in this book.

200 g sugar
4 egg yolks
95 g cornflour
1 litre milk
1 vanilla stick
10 speculoos biscuits

- Mix 100 g of sugar with the egg yolks and cornflour.
- Add a little milk to give a smooth mixture.
- Bring the remaining milk to the boil with the rest of the sugar and the vanilla stick.
- Add the egg mixture to the boiling milk and boil thoroughly.
- Rinse out a pudding mould and place a small layer of the pudding mix into the mould.
- Break the speculoos biscuits into large pieces and place on top.
- Pour the remaining pudding mix over the biscuits.
- Cover and leave to cool.
- Turn out onto a dish before serving.

Tip: want a thinner pudding?
Use an extra 250 ml of milk and pour into individual moulds.
This version forms the basis for the apple tartlets on p. 87.

SPECULOOS CREAM PUFFS

These puffs are perfect for Sunday afternoon coffee. Don't make them too long in advance, because the cream makes the puffs go soft.

FOR 50 PUFFS 200 ml water 100 g butter 150 g flour 5 or 6 eggs 400 ml whipping cream (at least 40% fat) 1 sachet of vanilla sugar 100 g ground speculoos	▪ Preheat the oven to 180 °C. ▪ Heat the water together with the butter over low heat until boiling. ▪ Remove the pan from the stove and stir in the flour with a wooden spoon. ▪ Return to the stove and continue stirring until the mixture is dry and no longer sticks to the pan. ▪ Remove the pan again from the stove and add an egg, stirring all the time. ▪ Add a second egg as soon as the mixture is evenly stirred. ▪ Repeat until all eggs are used. ▪ If the mixture is still too thick to squeeze out (for this it must be not quite runny), then add another half an egg. ▪ Place the dough into a pastry bag with a size 11 tip. ▪ Squeeze the puffs out onto a baking tray lined with baking paper, leaving sufficient distance between each puff. ▪ Bake for about 20 minutes until golden. ▪ Remove from the oven and leave to cool on a wire rack. ▪ Whip the cream firmly with the sugar. ▪ Add the crushed biscuits and mix with a spatula. ▪ Cut the cooled puffs in half crossways and fill them using a spoon. ▪ Serve immediately.

Tip: unfilled puffs can be kept in the freezer. Vacuum pack them and after thawing place for 1 minute in a hot oven to make them crispy again.

FRANGIPANE AND SPECULOOS TART

For the yeast pastry
40 g fresh yeast
120 ml lukewarm water
400 g flour
1 egg
20 g sugar
80 g butter
8 g salt

For the frangipane filling
250 g butter at room temperature
250 g sugar
250 g ground almonds
4 eggs
75 g flour

For the speculoos macaroons
See recipe on p. 90

- Dissolve the yeast in the water.
- Mix with the remaining ingredients, without adding the salt.
- Add the salt only at the end when you have a smooth dough.
- Knead the dough into a ball, cover with foil and leave to rest.
- For the filling beat the butter and sugar into a white, airy mass.
- Add the ground almonds and mix well.
- Add the eggs one by one and mix again after each egg.
- Once you have a smooth mixture, add the flour and fold it in briefly.
- Preheat the oven to 180 °C.
- Line a baking tin with baking paper and cover the bottom and sides with the pastry dough.
- Press the speculoos macaroons flat and cover the bottom of the tart with them until no more pastry is visible.
- Pour the frangipane filling on the macaroons.
- Bake for 30 minutes.
- Leave to cool.
- For a frosted finish, spread with a mixture of water and icing sugar.

MARZIPAN AND SPECULOOS CAKELETS

FOR 25 CAKES

100 g butter
3 eggs
125 g marzipan
40 g icing sugar
75 g flour
5 g baking powder
1/4 teaspoon speculoos spices

- Preheat the oven to 200 °C.
- Grease well a cupcake baking tin.
- Mix the butter until white and airy.
- Mix an egg into the marzipan and the icing sugar.
- Add the mixture to the butter and mix well.
- Add the remaining eggs one by one.
- Sift the flour with the baking powder and spices and fold into the dough.
- Use a pastry bag to place the dough into the cake tin.
- Bake for 12 minutes and leave to cool before removing from the tin.

Tip: use 50/50 marzipan. If you can't find this, replace it with 60 g of powdered almonds (very finely ground almonds) and 60 g sugar.

CHEESE AND SPECULOOS TART

It's the topping poured on at the end that gives this tart its very special taste.

For the base
80 g butter
150 g rough-ground speculoos

For the filling
250 g ricotta
250 g cream cheese
300 g sugar
5 large eggs
60 g white chocolate
60 g very finely ground speculoos
1 pinch of speculoos spices

For the topping
200 g sour cream
2 tablespoons sugar
3 tablespoons strong coffee
cinnamon (depending on taste)

- Preheat the oven to 170 °C.
- Grease a 22 cm springform baking tin and cover the bottom with baking paper.
- Melt the butter and mix with the ground speculoos.
- Distribute over the bottom of the springform and press down well with the back of a spoon.
- Place in the refrigerator.
- Mix the ricotta, cream cheese and sugar until smooth.
- Add the eggs one by one, beating well each time.
- Melt the chocolate and mix into the dough.
- Add the ground speculoos and spices.
- Pour the mixture into the springform and bake for 60 minutes.
- Mix the sour cream with the sugar and coffee.
- Add cinnamon to taste.
- Spread the topping over the tart while still warm and bake another 5 minutes at 150 °C.
- With a knife, loose the tart from the sides of the springform, but don't remove the tin yet.
- Leave to cool for at least 2 hours in the refrigerator.

Tip: try and make this cake one day in advance, as it tastes even better after spending the whole night in the refrigerator.

SPECULOOS AND LIME SLICE

This sounds like a strange combination, but the tangy taste of lime with speculoos is a divine combination. A dessert for winter and summer, but prepare enough of them, because no one will refuse a second helping.

FOR 5 SLICES

6 gelatine leaves
100 ml lime juice
100 g egg white
150 g icing sugar
500 ml cream (at least 40% fat)
250 g speculoos dough

- Soak the gelatine for ten minutes and squeeze out well.
- Heat the lime juice and stir in the squeezed-out gelatine.
- Stir until the gelatine is completely dissolved and put on one side.
- Beat the egg white and sugar together until stiff.
- With a beater, mix the cooled lime juice into the egg white.
- Whip the cream to a thick liquid consistency and then fold carefully into the egg white mixture.
- Cover a rectangular bowl with plenty of plastic foil, leaving the foil hanging over the sides.
- Pour the lemon mousse into the bowl and place in the freezer for several hours.
- Roll out the speculoos dough as thin as possible.
- Cut into fifteen rectangles, bake and cool.
- Take the frozen mousse out of the bowl with the help of the foil overhangs.
- Take a speculoos rectangle and cut the mousse to size.
- Lay a biscuit on each side of the piece of mousse and then cut the mousse in half along its full length.
- Continue until you have the chosen thickness of mousse.
- Make slices in this way, cleaning the sides for a smart, regular shape.
- Leave for a quarter of an hour before serving, so that the speculoos is slightly moistened by the thawing mousse.

CUPCAKES WITH SPECULOOS TOPPING

A Belgian twist to the cupcake.

FOR 12 CAKES

For the cupcakes
125 g granulated sugar
125 g butter
2 eggs
125 g self-raising flour
2 tablespoons milk

For the topping
75 g egg white
150 g sugar
225 g butter (at room temperature, cut into small blocks)
100 g ground speculoos
speculoos spices (optional)

- Preheat the oven to 160 to 180 °C, depending on the type of oven.
- Line a muffin tray with twelve paper cups.
- Cream the sugar and butter for the cupcakes until smooth.
- Add the eggs one by one.
- Add the flour and mix briefly into a smooth dough.
- Add the milk last and blend in briefly until the milk has been absorbed.
- Fill the cake cups three quarters full, using a pastry bag.
- Bake for about 22 minutes; the cakes are ready when nothing sticks to a toothpick or wooden skewer.
- For the topping beat the egg whites and sugar lightly with a whisk.
- Then continue beating in the bain-marie until the sugar is fully dissolved.
- Pour the mixture into the bowl of the food processor and beat with the whisk at medium speed until the mixture has become stiff and the bowl feels cold on the outside.
- Replace the whisk with the mixer's K-beater and add the butter block by block. The mixture will first be grainy and then look as if it's going to curdle, but that's normal, just continue beating until you have a smooth mixture.
- Stir the ground speculoos into the topping and add further spices if desired.
- Using a pastry bag, spiral the topping onto the cupcakes and decorate with a piece of speculoos biscuit.

SPECULOOS CAKES WITH BANANA

FOR 40 CAKES

200 g butter at room temperature
200 g brown sugar
5 eggs
175 g cornflour
90 g flour
5 g baking powder
5 g salt
50 g caramel with speculoos
   (see recipe on p. 31)
2 bananas

- Preheat the oven to 160 °C.
- Beat the butter and sugar together into an airy mass.
- Add the eggs one by one.
- Sift and mix in the cornflour, flour, baking powder and salt.
- Then beat the caramel into the dough.
- Grease a small muffin tin and half-fill the cups with the dough.
- Place a thin slice of banana on top of each cake.
- Bake for 13 to 14 minutes at 190 °C.

Tip: use very ripe bananas, otherwise the cakes will taste a little bitter.

SPECULOOS MOUSSE WITH VANILLA AND WHIPPED CHOCOLATE CREAM

FOR 5 GLASSES

100 g quark (soft curd cheese)
100 g ground speculoos
2 egg whites
100 g vanilla speculoos
150 ml whipped cream
1 sachet of vanilla sugar
30 g dark chocolate

- Beat the quark until light and airy and mix with the ground speculoos.
- Beat the egg whites until stiff and fold very gently into the mixture.
- Divide the mixture between five glasses and leave for 2 hours to stiffen.
- Break the vanilla speculoos biscuits into pieces and distribute over the mousse.
- Whip the cream with the vanilla sugar until stiff.
- Break the chocolate into very small pieces.
- Fold the chocolate into the whipped cream.
- Divide the cream among the glasses and serve immediately.

SPECULOOS KRAMIEK

The Flemish version of brioche. Bake a sufficient number of loaves, because after one slice you'll come back for another and another ...

FOR 2 BIG OR 4 SMALL LOAVES

25 g fresh yeast
220 ml milk
2 eggs
550 g flour
125 g soft butter
10 g salt
25 g sugar
200 g speculoos

- Dissolve the yeast in the slightly warmed milk.
- Mix one egg with the flour and pour in the milk.
- Knead well, then cover the bowl with a clean cloth and leave the dough to rise to double its volume.
- Beat the air out of the dough.
- Cut the butter into small lumps and work into the dough together with the salt and the sugar.
- Knead into a pliable dough that no longer sticks to the work surface.
- Let the dough rise until it has doubled in size again.
- Beat the air out of the dough.
- Divide the dough into two halves, and put aside 100 g from each half.
- Roll out one of the halves into a long, narrow strip, of the same width as the speculoos biscuits.
- Place one biscuit across the end of the dough strip.
- Turn over the dough onto it and place another speculoos onto the dough.
- Continue concertina-wise, dough layer-speculoos-dough layer etc., until you reach the end of the strip.
- Roll out one of the 100 g pieces of dough into a long thin strip and wrap it round the filled dough mass.
- Repeat for the second half of the dough.
- Place in a greased rectangular baking pan and leave to rise.
- Brush the top with a loosely beaten egg.
- Leave to rise for a further 45 minutes.
- Bake for around 25 minutes at 180 °C.

You can also divide the dough into two halves. Roll out one half and top with ground speculoos. Roll out the other half and lay on top of the first half. Roll up the lot and place in a baking tin.

LEMON MERINGUE TART

crumble pastry
1 tin of sweetened condensed milk (397 g)
3 egg yolks
1 egg
120 g lemon juice
100 g quark (soft curd cheese)
100 g ground speculoos
150 g egg white
300 g sugar

- Preheat the oven to 180 °C.
- Cover a mould with the crumble pastry and bake blind for ten minutes.
- Beat the condensed milk with the egg yolks and the egg into a smooth mixture.
- Add the lemon juice and quark and mix in with the rest.
- Distribute the ground speculoos over the crumble base and press down firmly.
- Spoon the filling carefully over the speculoos.
- Bake the tart for 15 minutes at 180 °C.
- Place the sugar and egg white in a small steel pan and heat, stirring all the time.
- Remove from the heat once the sugar is fully dissolved.
- Beat until cold in the stand mixer. As soon as the mixture is shiny and forms peaks, it is ready.
- Spread the egg white-sugar mixture over the baked lemon tart and tap it to form peaks.
- Colour the meringue for 30 seconds under the grill.

Tip: stay next to the grill. Once a meringue begins to colour, things move very fast.

SPECULOOS RISOTTO

My interpretation of the famous rice pudding.

400 ml milk
70 g broken speculoos
1 pinch of cinnamon
30 g butter
100 g risotto rice (carnaroli)
80 g demerara sugar
1 tablespoon mascarpone
50 g speculoos

- Bring the milk to the boil with 50 grams of broken speculoos.
- Stir in the cinnamon and set aside.
- Melt the butter in a large heavy-bottomed saucepan.
- Add the rice and cook for two minutes, stirring continuously.
- Then add in 100 ml of the speculoos milk and stir until completely absorbed by the rice.
- Add another soupspoon of speculoos milk and stir until completely absorbed by the rice.
- Continue in this way until the rice is al dente and creamy.
- Stir the sugar and the mascarpone into the rice and leave to cool.
- Just before serving, add in the remaining 20 grams of broken speculoos.

Tip: for this recipe use only real risotto rice, it really does not work well with ordinary rice.

SPECULOOS ICE CREAM CUPCAKES

FOR 1 LITRE OF SPECULOOS ICE CREAM

500 ml milk
150 ml cream
115 g sugar
40 g glucose
4 egg yolks
200 g ground speculoos
1 pinch of speculoos spices
1 coffee spoon of speculoos paste with
caramel

FOR 12 CUPCAKES

125 g granulated sugar
125 g butter
2 eggs
125 g self-raising flour
1 teaspoon vanilla essence
2 tablespoons milk

FOR THE SPECULOOS ICE CREAM
- Heat the milk and cream briefly over medium heat.
- Beat the sugar, glucose and egg yolks together into a white mixture. Stir in a little warm milk. Beat to prevent curdling.
- Add the remaining milk in the same way little by little.
- Bind the mixture by heating over medium heat to 82 °C. It must absolutely not boil, so keep a careful eye on the temperature!
- Pour through a sieve and mix to a smooth consistency with the fat balls as small as possible.
- Cool the mixture as fast as possible on an ice bed to around 6 °C.
- Leave to mature for at least 12 hours in the refrigerator.
- Mix the ground speculoos with the spices and fold into the mixture.
- Mix in the speculoos paste.
- Process according to the ice machine manufacturer's instructions.

- Preheat the oven to 160 to 180 °C, depending on the type of oven.
- Mix the sugar and butter until even.
- Add the eggs one by one.
- Then add the flour and vanilla essence and mix briefly into a smooth dough.
- Add the milk and mix briefly until the milk is absorbed.
- Using a pastry bag, three quarters fill the greased little moulds.
- Bake for around 22 minutes. The cupcakes are ready when nothing sticks to the toothpick or wooden skewer.
- Let them cool and take out of the tin.
- Hollow out the cupcakes very carefully and fill them with the ice cream.
- Serve immediately.

LAYERED MERINGUE TART

2 egg whites
125 g dark muscovado sugar
1 pinch of speculoos spices
300 ml whipped cream
150 g speculoos

- Preheat the oven to 100 °C.
- Beat the egg whites until stiff in an absolutely fat-free bowl.
- Mix the sugar with the speculoos spices.
- Add the sugar mixture spoonful by spoonful to the egg white and continue beating till it holds peaks.
- Draw three circles on a sheet of baking paper. Then with a pastry bag form the meringue into disk shapes.
- Bake for 2 hours in the oven.
- Beat the whipping cream until stiff and spread thickly over the three disks.
- Sprinkle broken speculoos biscuit over each disk.
- Pile the three disks on top of each other and serve immediately.

APPLE TARTLETS WITH SPECULOOS

FOR 12 TARTLETS

12 square sheets of puff pastry
12 coffee spoons of ground almonds
12 coffee spoons of sugar
500 g vanilla pudding
   (see recipe on p. 58)
120 g ground speculoos
6 apples
10 g butter
1 pinch of cinnamon

- Preheat the oven to 200 °C.
- Line 12 greased and floured mini-moulds with the puff pastry.
- Prick the bottom with a fork.
- Mix the almond powder and sugar and cover the bottom of the moulds with a thin layer to form a moisture barrier.
- Three quarters fill the moulds with vanilla pudding.
- Place a layer of crushed biscuits on top of the vanilla pudding.
- Peel half an apple for each tartlet and decorate as you wish.
- Mix the butter with the cinnamon, melt and brush over the apples.
- Bake for 22 minutes.
- Leave to cool in the mould.

SPECULOOS PASTE CAKES

FOR 20 CAKES

125 g butter at room temperature
125 g dark muscovado sugar
2 eggs
2 tablespoons milk
125 g self-raising flour
100 g ground speculoos
100 g speculoos paste made with white chocolate
sugar

- Preheat the oven to 170 °C.
- Beat the butter and sugar until airy.
- Add the eggs one at a time, beating well each time.
- Mix in the milk.
- Finally, add the flour and mix briefly.
- Fill the cake tins one third full with the cake mix.
- Cover with ground speculoos and a spoonful of speculoos paste.
- Fill up (to three quarters full) with the cake mix.
- Bake for 30 minutes and cool in the tins.
- Sprinkle with sugar and serve.

Tip: you can also use speculoos paste with caramel taste (see recipe on p. 31).

SPECULOOS MACAROONS

This delicacy combines the typical structure of a soft macaroon with the classic speculoos taste to give a surprising effect.

FOR 50 MACAROONS

135 g sugar
135 g finely ground almonds
6 g speculoos spices
90 g flour
270 g icing sugar
150 g egg white
10 g ground speculoos

- Preheat the oven to 175 °C.
- Mix the sugar, almonds and speculoos spices.
- Add the flour and icing sugar and mix well.
- Add the egg white slowly, beating all the time into a homogeneous mixture.
- Using a pastry bag, place little blobs of mixture on a baking tray covered with baking paper.
- Leave sufficient room between the macaroons, as they expand a bit.
- Sprinkle lightly with ground speculoos.
- Bake for 14 to 15 minutes.
- Store in a plastic container.

SPECULOOS AND WHITE CHOCOLATE TART

50 g butter
200 g ground speculoos
35 ml water
70 g sugar
1 leaf gelatine
200 g white chocolate
500 ml whipped cream
   (at least 40% fat)
3 egg yolks
white chocolate shavings

- Place a stainless steel ring without a base onto a sheet of plastic foil.
- Cut out a strip of baking paper and line the inside of the ring, if necessary using baking spray to hold it in place.
- Melt the butter and mix with 150 grams of ground speculoos.
- Distribute this mixture over the base of the ring and press firm with the back of a spoon.
- Place in the refrigerator.
- Boil the water and add the sugar; keep stirring until the sugar is dissolved.
- Set aside to cool.
- Soak the gelatine five minutes in cold water and squeeze well.
- Melt the chocolate in a bain-marie.
- Add the squeezed-out gelatine and stir until dissolved.
- Whip the cream to a thick liquid consistency.
- Add a little whipping cream to the chocolate and mix well.
- Pour the partially cooled sugar water over the egg yolks and mix well.
- Fold into the whipping cream/chocolate mixture.
- Then add the remaining whipping cream.
- Pour the mixture onto the speculoos base and leave in the refrigerator to stiffen for at least 6 hours.
- Carefully remove the ring and then the baking paper.
- Decorate the side of the tart with the rest of the ground speculoos.
- Finally sprinkle the chocolate shavings over the tart.

SPECULOOS AND CARAMEL CAKE

1 can sweetened condensed milk (397 g)
200 g butter at room temperature
200 g dark muscovado sugar
3 eggs
200 g self-raising flour
15 g speculoos spices
almond shavings

- Place the unopened can of milk into a saucepan of water and bring to the boil.
- Boil for at least 3 hours, adding water regularly, so that the can is always under water.
- Leave to cool for at least a full night before opening the can!
- Preheat the oven to 160 °C.
- Beat the butter and sugar together into an airy mass.
- Add one egg and beat until smooth.
- Repeat with the other eggs.
- Sift the flour and speculoos spices into the mixture and mix till smooth.
- Pour into a greased turban cake mould.
- Bake for 55 minutes and then check with a toothpick or wooden skewer whether the cake is ready.
- Leave to cool and then remove the baking tin.
- Place the cake on a dish, open the can of milk and pour over the cake.
- Decorate with a handful of sliced almonds.

Tip: the caramel is also delicious without the cake ... simply with a spoon.

SPECULOOS AND CURD CHEESE BAVAROIS WITH RASPBERRY COULIS

You can also replace the raspberries with mango.

For the base
80 g butter
150 g rough-ground speculoos

For the filling
4 gelatine leaves
juice of 1/2 a lemon
2 egg yolks
80 g sugar
200 g quark (soft curd cheese)
250 ml whipping cream (at least 40% fat)
1 handful of raspberries

- Place a stainless steel ring without a base onto a sheet of plastic foil.
- Cut out a strip of baking paper and line the inside of the ring with it, if necessary using baking spray to keep it in place.
- Melt the butter and mix with the ground speculoos.
- Distribute the mixture over the base of the ring and press firm with the back of a spoon.
- Place in the refrigerator.
- Soak the gelatine for five minutes in cold water and squeeze well.
- Heat the lemon juice and add the squeezed gelatine.
- Stir until gelatine is completely dissolved and leave to cool.
- Beat the egg yolks with 40 grams of sugar.
- Add the quark and beat well.
- Add in the cooled lemon juice and beat again briskly.
- Whip the cream firmly with the remaining sugar and fold into the quark mixture.
- Pour the mixture onto the speculoos base and leave to stiffen in the refrigerator for at least 6 hours.
- Carefully remove the ring and then remove the baking paper.
- Mix the raspberries and strain through a sieve to remove the seeds.
- Thicken the coulis if desired by heating with a little sugar.
- Spread this carefully over the top of the tart before serving and also decorate the dish with a few droplets.

Tip: you can also stiffen the tart in the freezer. This is faster and makes the ring and baking paper easier to remove.

SPECULOOS WHOOPIES

Move over cupcake, here comes the whoopie pie!

FOR 35 WHOOPIES

For the whoopies
140 g butter
150 g dark muscovado sugar
1 egg
75 ml soft candy syrup
75 ml ginger syrup
480 g flour
1 teaspoon speculoos spices
1 pinch of salt
1 teaspoon baking powder
150 ml buttermilk

For the filling
50 g butter
300 g icing sugar
25 ml cream (at least 40% fat)
50 g ground speculoos

- Preheat the oven to 170 °C.
- Beat the butter and sugar into an airy mass.
- Add the egg and beat until smooth.
- Mix in the candy syrup and ginger.
- Sift in the flour with the spices, salt and baking powder and mix till everything is absorbed.
- Then beat in the buttermilk and blend to a smooth dough.
- With a tablespoon, place little dollops of dough onto a baking tray lined with baking paper.
- Leave enough space between the dollops as they expand outwards during baking.
- Bake for 10 to 12 minutes: when ready the whoopies will rise back when you press them.
- Mix the butter smoothly with the icing sugar.
- Add the cream and beat into a smooth butter cream.
- Fold the ground speculoos into the cream.
- Using a pastry bag, cover half the whoopies with a blob of butter cream and cover with the other half.

COFFEE-COATED SPECULOOS SPONGE CAKE

Most of us have one time or another dunked their speculoos biscuit in their coffee, so a filling for this fluffy sponge was quickly found.

For the sponge cake
5 eggs
4 egg yolks
250 g sugar
200 g flour
1 pinch speculoos spices

For the speculoos paste
200 g speculoos
1/2 cup coffee with milk
cinnamon

For the butter cream
200 ml milk
200 g sugar
2 egg yolks
500 g butter at room temperature
ground coffee
20 g ground speculoos

Tip: this speculoos paste is also delicious on sandwiches. Keep in the refrigerator and use within three days.

- Preheat the oven to 180 °C.
- Beat the eggs and egg yolks in a bain-marie until frothy.
- Place the egg mixture in the stand mixer and beat until cold again.
- Carefully fold in the sugar, flour and spices. Beat at little as possible in order to keep the air in the dough.
- Grease a mould and dust with flour.
- Bake the sponge for around 30 to 35 minutes at 190 °C; use a toothpick or wooden skewer to check whether the cake is ready.
- Remove from the mould and leave to cool.
- For the speculoos paste break the speculoos into pieces and pour with the coffee into a bowl.
- Add a little cinnamon and set aside.
- For the butter cream, mix the milk, sugar and egg yolks.
- Heat, stirring all the time, to 82 ° C and then leave to cool.
- Mix in the butter.
- If desired for taste, stir some ground coffee into the butter cream.
- Place half the butter cream into a bowl and set aside.
- Stir the speculoos paste well to produce an even mush, press well and remove any excess moisture.
- Carefully cut the cooled sponge in half.
- Cover the bottom half with the speculoos paste.
- Place the upper half back on top.
- Now take the coffee-butter cream and spread over the side and top of the sponge with a palette knife.
- Place the remaining cream in a pastry bag and use it to decorate the top of the sponge.
- Cover the side with ground speculoos, the top with ground coffee and serve.

HAPPY GINGER CAKE

The inspiration for the cheerful little flowers on this cake I took from a Sweet Spring Cake made by a friend and which made me immediately feel happy. Sofie, thank you for letting me borrow your decoration idea for this book.

185 g butter at room temperature
185 g demerara sugar
3 eggs
2 tablespoons ginger syrup
185 g self-raising flour
100 g ginger speculoos
   (see recipe on p. 26)
2 tablespoons icing sugar
little marzipan or sugar paste flowers

- Preheat the oven to 155 °C.
- Beat the butter and sugar to an airy consistency.
- Add the eggs one at a time, beating each time until smooth.
- Mix in the ginger syrup.
- Add the flour and mix into an smooth dough.
- Crumble the ginger biscuit and fold it into the dough.
- Spoon this into a well buttered and floured mould.
- Bake for 40 minutes and check with a toothpick or wooden skewer whether the cake is ready.
- Leave to cool in the mould.
- For the frosting mix the icing sugar with a little water, adding more water until the frosting is the desired consistency.
- Pour the frosting over the cake and decorate immediately with little marzipan or sugar paste flowers.

SPECULOOS CHEESECAKE

FOR 12 CHEESECAKES

90 g butter
120 g ground speculoos
150 g cream cheese
120 g ricotta
25 g flour
125 g sugar
1 pinch of salt
2 eggs
1 egg yolk

- Preheat the oven to 170 °C.
- Melt 60 grams of butter and mix with the ground speculoos.
- Line a muffin tray with twelve paper cups, divide the speculoos mixture between them, press down well and refrigerate.
- Mix the cream cheese with the ricotta.
- Sift the flour with the sugar and salt into the cheese mixture and beat briskly.
- Beat in the eggs and the egg yolk to give an even mixture.
- Melt the remaining butter and briefly mix in.
- Fill the paper cases to just below the rim with the cheese cake mix.
- Place the muffin tray at the bottom of the oven.
- Bake for 5 minutes at 170 °C and another 15 minutes at 150 °C.
- Leave the cakes to cool, cover with foil and place in the refrigerator till the next day.

SPECULOOS BREAD PUDDING

200 g stale bread
200 g speculoos (type at your choice)
800 ml milk
150 g dark muscovado sugar
120 g demerara sugar
1 sachet of vanilla sugar
3 eggs

- Cut the crusts off the bread and break the speculoos biscuits into pieces.
- Put everything into a deep bowl and pour in the milk.
- Sprinkle the sugar over the mixture.
- Leave to soak for 2 hours, stirring occasionally.
- Preheat the oven to 180 °C.
- If you want, break down any remaining pieces to leave a thick mush.
- Whisk the eggs and stir into the mush.
- Sprinkle the vanilla sugar on top and stir briskly.
- Pour the mixture into a greased baking dish.
- Bake for 45 to 50 minutes.
- Leave to cool and serve with coffee.

Tip: always use at least 50% of bread for this recipe, otherwise the pudding becomes far too heavy and dry.

SPECULOOS BUTTER CREAM BISCUITS

Based on our popular bokkepootje *(billy goat's hoof), but in a round shape.*

FOR 50 BISCUITS

For the vanilla biscuit
415 g sugar
5 egg whites
225 g ground almonds.
50 g flour
25 g rice meal

For the butter cream
200 ml milk
200 g sugar
2 egg yolks
500 g butter at room temperature
80 g ground speculoos
20 g chocolate

- Beat 190 g of the sugar with the egg whites to a foam.
- Mix the remaining sugar with the ground almonds.
- Then add the flour and rice meal to the almond-sugar mixture and fold briefly into the foam.
- Place blobs of mixture onto a baking tray with a pastry bag.
- Space wide enough apart, because they run out.
- Bake for 18 minutes at 185 °C in a pre-heated oven.
- For the butter cream, mix the milk, sugar and egg yolks.
- Heat the mixture, stirring all the time, to 82 °C and then leave to cool.
- Mix in the butter.
- Stir the ground speculoos into the butter cream.
- Using a pastry bag, apply speculoos butter cream to half of the biscuits and cover with the other half.
- Melt the chocolate and decorate with a few lines of chocolate.

Tip: these biscuits are perfect for freezing. Place them in a plastic box and take them out of the freezer one hour before serving.

SPECULOOS AND PEAR SYRUP TART

Sirop de Liège is a typical Belgian product I like to work with. The combination with speculoos is not immediately obvious, but it works wonderfully.

For the tart
6 eggs
325 g butter
330 g dark muscovado sugar
330 g self-raising flour
100 g very roughly ground speculoos

For the filling
75 g egg white
150 g sugar
225 g butter (at room temperature cut into small blocks)
4 tablespoons Sirop de Liège *

- Preheat the oven to 160 °C.
- Separate the eggs.
- Mix the egg yolks with the butter and sugar and beat well.
- Sift the flour into the mixture and mix.
- Whisk the egg whites by hand until frothy, add to the dough and mix thoroughly.
- Fold in the ground speculoos.
- Bake for 45 minutes and then check with a toothpick or wooden skewer whether the cake is ready.
- Leave to cool.
- For the filling, beat the egg white and sugar lightly with a whisk.
- Then continue beating it in the bain-marie until the sugar is fully dissolved.
- Pour the mixture into the bowl of the food processor and beat with the whisk at medium speed until the mixture has become stiff and the bowl feels cold on the outside.
- Replace the whisk with the mixer's K-beater and add the butter block by block. The mixture will first be grainy and then look like it's going to curdle, but that's normal, just continue beating until you have a smooth mixture.
- Heat 2 tablespoons of Sirop de Liège until slightly liquid.
- Let the syrup cool slightly and then beat into the butter mixture.
- Cut the speculoos cake open, apply the filling generously to the bottom half and place the upper half back on top.
- Melt another 2 tablespoons of Sirop de Liège until slightly liquid and spread immediately over the top of the tart.

(*) Sirop de Liège is a typical Belgian syrup made of pears, apples and dates. It has a very distinctive taste and cannot be replaced by anything else ...

SPECULOOS FUDGE

A soft caramel that does not stick to the teeth.

FOR **1.3** KG OF FUDGE

500 g sugar
115 g butter
2 tablespoons Lyle's Golden Syrup
120 ml milk
1 tin of evaporated milk (400 g)
100 g white chocolate
30 ml whisky (optional)
100 g speculoos, broken into large pieces

- Mix the sugar, butter, Golden Syrup and milk in a heavy-bottomed steel pan, and bring to the boil, stirring all the time.
- Turn down the heat and leave to simmer for 30 minutes.
- Add the white chocolate and stir until melted.
- If desired, the whisky can be added at this stage.
- Cover a shallow baking dish with baking paper. Pour half of the liquid fudge into the dish.
- Cover with the speculoos pieces.
- Pour the rest of the fudge over the speculoos and leave to cool.
- Cut the fudge into squares.

Tip: this fudge keeps well for weeks and is also perfect for freezing.

ORANGE CAKES

FOR 35 CAKES

3 eggs
160 g butter
165 g demerara sugar
165 g self-raising flour
50 g finely ground speculoos
50 g candied orange

- Preheat the oven to 170 °C.
- Separate the eggs.
- Mix the egg yolks with the butter and sugar and beat well.
- Sift in the flour and mix.
- Whisk the egg whites by hand until frothy.
- Add them to the mixture and mix everything thoroughly.
- Fold in the fine-ground speculoos.
- Cut the candied orange into small pieces, keeping back a few pieces as decoration.
- Use a pastry bag to place the dough into the cake tins.
- Decorate with pieces of candied orange.
- Bake for 18 minutes. The cakes are ready when a toothpick or wooden skewer comes out clean.

Tip: if you want you can put in two tablespoons of orange juice before adding the egg white.

PANCAKES WITH SPECULOOS BUTTER

I normally breakfast only lightly, but if I'm in New York, I simply have to have pancakes for breakfast, every day. With maple syrup and blueberries and lots of butter. My normal pancakes are served with speculoos butter, the speculoos version with a spoonful of candy syrup.

For the speculoos butter
25 g butter
15 g ground speculoos

For the pancakes
135 g self-raising flour
30 g dark sugar candy
1 egg
30 g melted butter
3 tablespoons milk
4 g speculoos spices for the speculoos pancakes
or
a pinch of salt for the normal pancakes
butter for baking

- Allow the butter for the speculoos butter to come up to room temperature and mix with the ground speculoos biscuits.
- Place in the refrigerator.
- Sift the flour into a bowl and add the sugar.
- Add the egg yolks and melted butter with the milk.
- Add the speculoos spices for the speculoos pancakes or the salt for the normal pancakes.
- Whisk the egg whites until stiff and fold gently into the dough.
- Heat a pan and melt a little butter in it.
- Place a spoonful of batter into the pan and let the pancake bake to a nice brown colour underneath.
- Turn over and let the other side brown nicely.
- For each new pancake, add a little butter to the pan.
- Serve the pancakes lukewarm with the speculoos butter and candy syrup.

SHOPPING LIST

Decoratiehuis Dali, Koning Ridderdijk 24-25, 8434 Westende, www.dali-matisse.be
Den Stal Interieurinrichting, Amerikalei 10-14, 2000 Antwerp, www.denstal.be
Dobs Koekietraps, www.dobs.be
Fou de Feu, Grote Kouterstraat 46, 9120 Vrasene, www.foudefeu.be
Habitat Antwerpen, GB shoppingcenter, Groenplaats, 2000 Antwerp, www.habitat.be
Kant Point de Rose, Wollestraat 27, 8000 Bruges, www.pointderose.be
Nono@Home, www.nonoathome.com
Sissy Boy, Nationalestraat 36, 2000 Antwerp, www.sissy-boy.be
Tafel van Amandine, Fruithoflaan 39, 2600 Berchem, www.tafelvanamandine.be
Wit + Goed table linen, www.witplusgoed.be

And to all friends, relatives, acquaintances and neighbours who allowed us to browse through their kitchen cupboards, a big thank you!

www.lannoo.com
Register on our website to receive a regular newsletter with information about new books and interesting, exclusive offers.

Juliette's Artisanale Koekenbakkerij
Wollestraat 31A – 8000 Bruges – Belgium
www.juliettes.be

TEXT & RECIPES: Brenda Keirsebilck and Katrien Vandamme
STYLING & PHOTOGRAPHY: Karen Van Winkel
IMAGE PROCESSING: Pixco
DESIGN: Leen Depooter – quod. voor de vorm.
ENGLISH TRANSLATION: Michael Lomax

If you have any comments or questions, please contact our editorial team at:
redactielifestyle@lannoo.com

© Uitgeverij Lannoo nv, Tielt, 2011
D/2011/45/613 – NUR 440-441
ISBN: 978 94 014 0011 4
Second printrun

All rights reserved. No part of this publication may be reproduced, stored in an automated database and/or published in any form or in any way, whether electronically, mechanically or in any other manner, without prior permission in writing from the publishers.